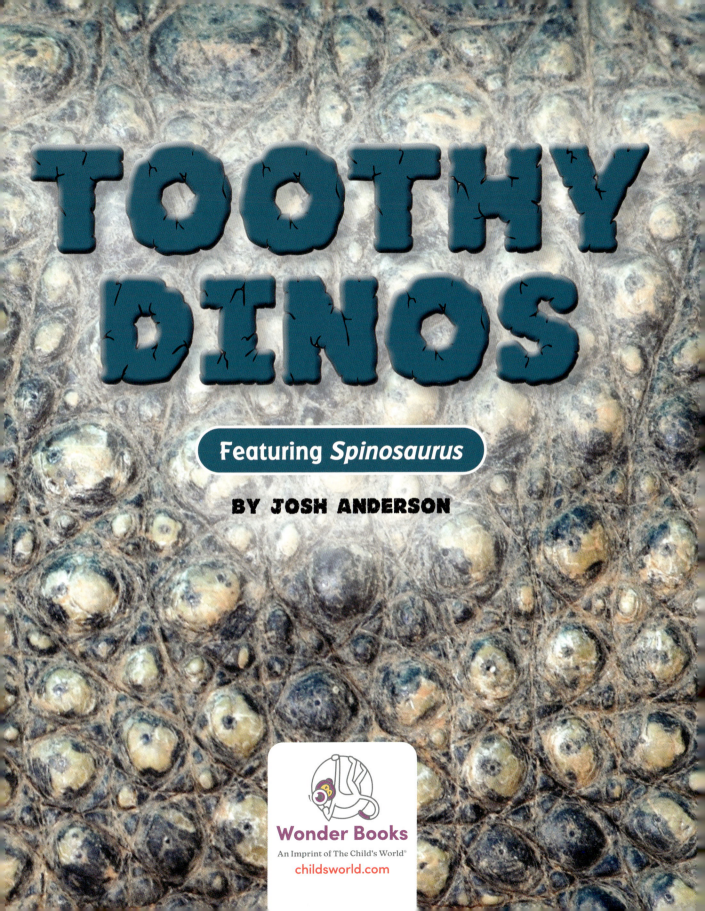

TOOTHY DINOS

Featuring *Spinosaurus*

BY JOSH ANDERSON

Wonder Books
An Imprint of The Child's World®
childsworld.com

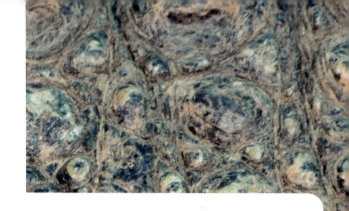

Published by The Child's World®
800-599-READ • www.childsworld.com

Copyright © 2023 by The Child's World®
All rights reserved. No part of this book may be reproduced or utilized in any form or by any means without written permission from the publisher.

Photography Credits
Cover: ©Vac1 / Getty Images; page 1: ©Pan Xunbin / Shutterstock; page 5: ©MR1805 / Getty Images; page 6: ©The Washington Post / Contributor / Getty Images; page 9: ©SAUL LOEB / Staff / Getty Images; page 10: ©Roberto Machado Noa / Contributor / Getty Images; page 11: ©dkvektor / Shutterstock; page 13: ©The Washington Post / Contributor / Getty Images; page 14: ©Marco Rubino / Shutterstock; page 15: ©Paulo Leite da Silva/Stocktrek Images / Getty Images; page 16: ©Tuul & Bruno Morandi / Getty Images; page 16: ©Julio Francisco; page 17: ©Julio Francisco; page 19: ©NurPhoto / Contributor / Getty Images; page 21: ©VANDERLEI ALMEIDA / Staff / Getty Images

ISBN Information
9781503865327 (Reinforced Library Binding)
9781503865945 (Portable Document Format)
9781503866782 (Online Multi-user eBook)
9781503867628 (Electronic Publication)

LCCN 2022940999

Printed in the United States of America

About the Author
Josh Anderson has published more than 50 books for children and young adults. His two sons, Leo and Dane, are the greatest joys in his life. Josh's hobbies include coaching youth basketball, no-holds-barred games of Exploding Kittens, reading, and family movie nights. His favorite dinosaur is a secret he'll never share!

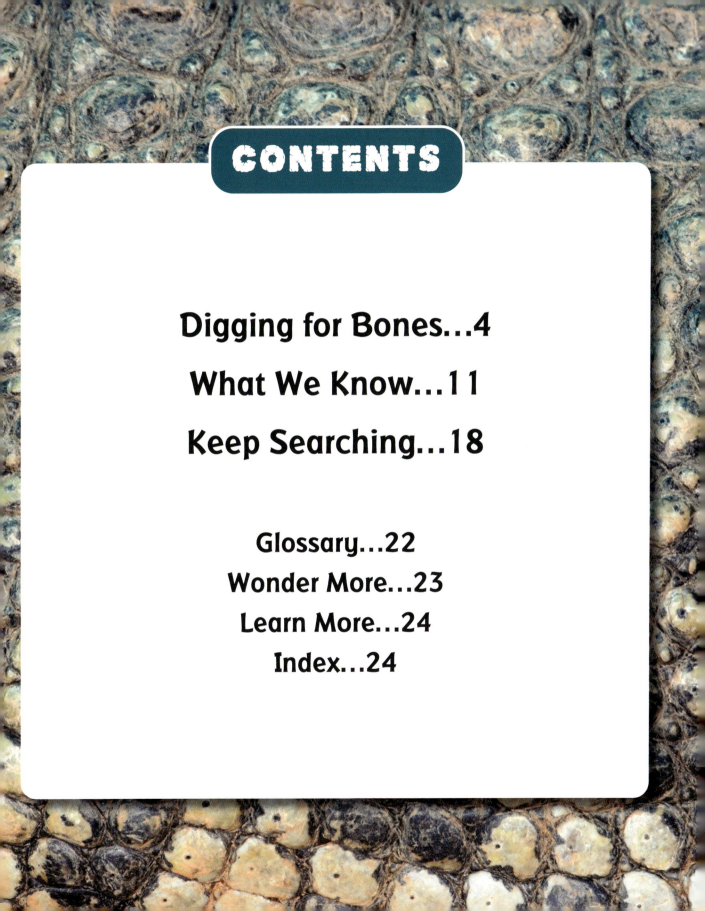

CONTENTS

Digging for Bones…4

What We Know…11

Keep Searching…18

Glossary…22
Wonder More…23
Learn More…24
Index…24

CHAPTER 1

Digging for Bones

Pretend you can time travel to a prehistoric age.... You've gone back about 95 million years to a beach in Northern Africa. You decide to dip your feet into the Mediterranean Sea. But you hear a loud sound behind you. Birds fly up into the air. A huge creature charges in your direction. Its jaws open up. You can see a set of terrifying, blade-like teeth. It has a huge ridge on its back that looks like the sail of a boat....

You have nowhere to hide. But the giant runs right past you! This **predator** has all the food it wants just past where you are standing. This is *Spinosaurus* (spyn-uh-SAWR-uss). You watch as the dinosaur gracefully dives into the water. Seconds later, you lose sight of it as it goes off to find a meal of whatever fish it can sink its teeth into.

How do we know so much about this swimming **carnivorous** dinosaur? The simple answer: SCIENCE! Let's learn more!

Spinosaurus had many knife-like teeth.

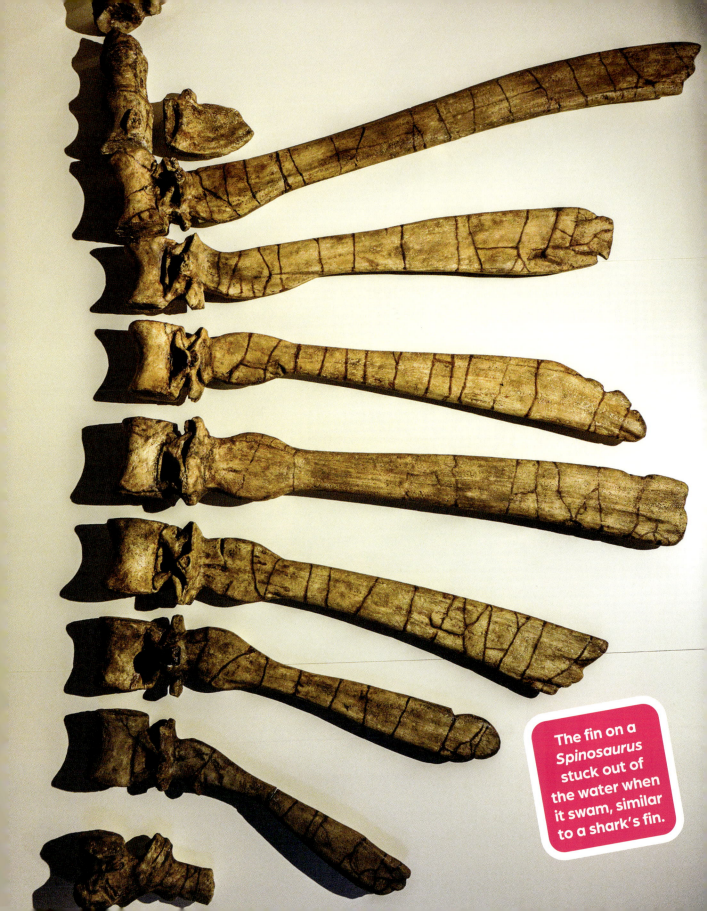

The fin on a *Spinosaurus* stuck out of the water when it swam, similar to a shark's fin.

Humans have been studying *Spinosaurus* for more than 100 years. The first *Spinosaurus* bones were found in Western Egypt in 1912. A German **paleontologist** named Ernst Stromer chose the name *Spinosaurus*. It means "spine lizard." Stromer pointed out some very unique things about *Spinosaurus*. He wrote that the dino had a longer, narrower snout than other big meat-eaters. And he wrote about the giant spines coming out of its back. Some parts of *Spinosaurus's* "sail" were 6.5 feet (2 meters) long.

The skeleton was kept in a German museum. The museum was bombed during World War II (1939–1945). The bones were destroyed. No other *Spinosaurus* skeleton was discovered for more than 70 years.

In 2008, a team of paleontologists discovered a new *Spinosaurus* skeleton in Morocco. Scientists could finally study *Spinosaurus* using modern tools.

They made many new discoveries about this fascinating dino. For the first time, a *Spinosaurus* tailbone was found. It was shaped differently from the tails of other large meat-eaters. This helped scientists figure out that *Spinosaurus* was semi-aquatic. This means it spent time both on land and in water. *Spinosaurus* is the only known semi-aquatic dinosaur!

Spinosaurus had nostrils near the top of its head, close to its eyes, which allowed it to breathe while swimming.

Spinosaurus probably weighed about as much as a military tank.

CHAPTER 2

What We Know

Spinosaurus was a **theropod**. Theropods were carnivorous dinosaurs who walked on two feet. They had three toes on each foot. *Spinosaurus* was the largest and heaviest of all carnivorous dinosaurs. It was bigger than *Tyrannosaurus rex* (teh-ran-uh-SAWR-uss REKS)!

When It Lived: 95 million years ago – The Late Cretaceous Period

First Discovered: 1912, Egypt

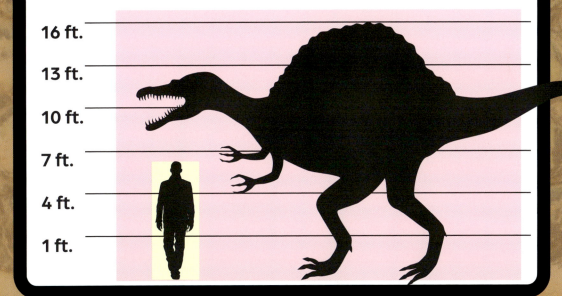

Spinosaurus ate mostly fish. But it also may have eaten other dinosaurs and pterosaurs. Pterosaurs were flying reptiles. They are related to dinosaurs. Scientists have found fish scales and the bones of other dinosaurs in its stomach. That is how they knew what Spinosaurus ate. They have also found *Spinosaurus* teeth inside of Pterosaur bones.

Most theropods walked only on their back two legs. But *Spinosaurus* had very long arms compared to its relatives. Some scientists think *Spinosaurus* preferred to walk on all fours at times.

FUN FACTS

- *Spinosaurus* lived at the same time and place as *Sarcosuchus* (sar-KAH-suk-uss), a huge prehistoric crocodile. They may have even done battle in the water!
- Scientists aren't sure about the purpose of the "sail" on *Spinosaurus's* back. It may have helped to regulate its body temperature.
- *Spinosaurus* has been described by some scientists as an "enormous river monster."
- The name *Spinosaurus* means "spine lizard."
- *Spinosaurus* was the scary, villainous dinosaur in the 2001 film *Jurassic Park 3*.

THEN AND NOW

For more than 100 years, no one had ever found a complete *Spinosaurus* tail. So scientists did what they often do when working with partial skeletons. They filled in the blanks based on what they know about other dinosaurs. But the tail found in a 2018 discovery showed something different than what the scientists expected. The tail was almost shaped like a fin. This was more proof that *Spinosaurus* spent its time in the water (see page 15).

Spinosaurus bones were dense, or heavy and compact, which helped it hunt underwater.

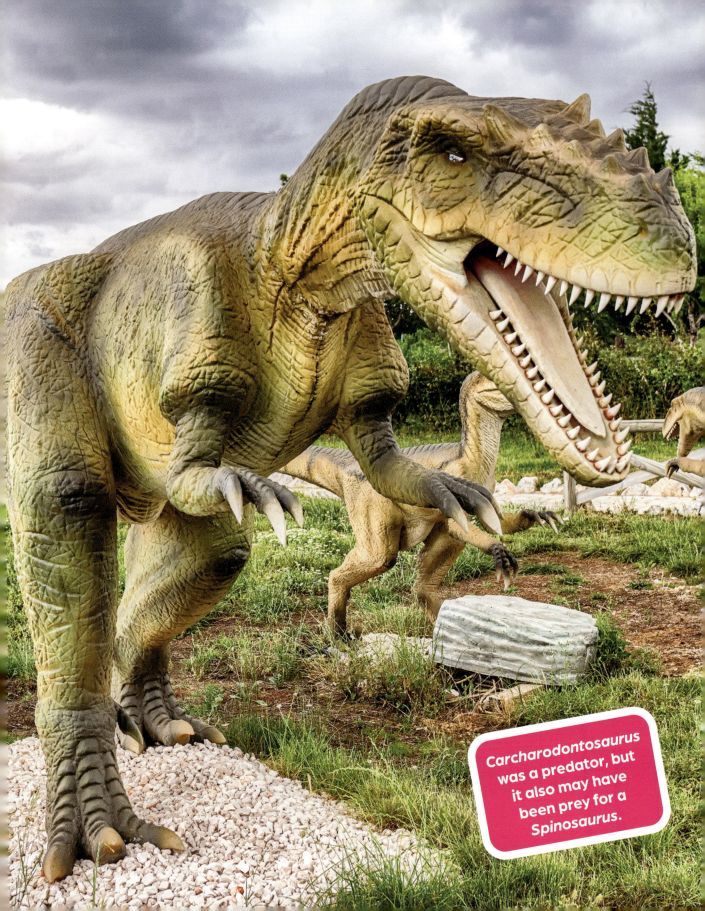

Carcharodontosaurus was a predator, but it also may have been prey for a Spinosaurus.

Spinosaurus wasn't the only dinosaur with a scary mouthful of sharp teeth. Here are some other predators from the ancient world.

Carcharodontosaurus (kar–kuh–roh–don–tuh–SAWR–uss) was another enormous carnivore that lived at the same time as *Spinosaurus*. *Carcharodontosaurus* also lived in Northern Africa. The two may have crossed paths.

Giganotosaurus (jy–gahn–oh–tuh–SAWR–uss) lived a bit earlier than *Spinosaurus*. It was found in South America. The "giant southern lizard" had a huge skull, strong arms with three clawed fingers, and very powerful back legs.

UP FOR DEBATE

Most paleontologists agree that *Spinosaurus* could swim, but not all of them agree that it could swim well. A 2020 study published in *Nature* magazine called *Spinosaurus* a "highly specialized aquatic predator." A more recent study states that it probably hunted in shallow water. It would stick part of its head underwater as it fished for prey. Perhaps the debate will be settled by the next discovery of a *Spinosaurus* skeleton.

SPINOSAURUS
(spyn-uh-SAWR-uss)

VS

Length: 50 feet (15 m)

Weight: 40,000 pounds (18,144 kilograms)

Top Speed: 15 miles (24 kilometers) per hour

Weakness: More suited for hunting fish than for hunting other dinos

Best Defense or Weapon: Ability to move on land or in water

GIGANOTOSAURUS
(jy-gahn-oh-tuh-SAWR-uss)

Length: 40 feet (12.2 m)

Weight: 16,000 pounds (7,257 kg)

Top Speed: 31 miles (50 km) per hour

Weakness: Fairly weak bite; small brain

Best Defense or Weapon: Flexible, three-clawed hands; hunted in packs

CHAPTER 3

Keep Searching

Modern tools did not exist when the first *Spinosaurus* was discovered in 1912. Today's paleontologists can learn much more from **fossils** than they could in the past. When another *Spinosaurus* skeleton was found in 2008, scientists were better equipped.

Scientists created a computer model of *Spinosaurus's* entire skeleton. One way scientists capture images to create computer models is to use an **electron microscope**. These can capture more details than microscopes of the past. After the bones are scanned, the pictures are turned into a computer model. Then scientists can examine the skeleton without actually touching the bones.

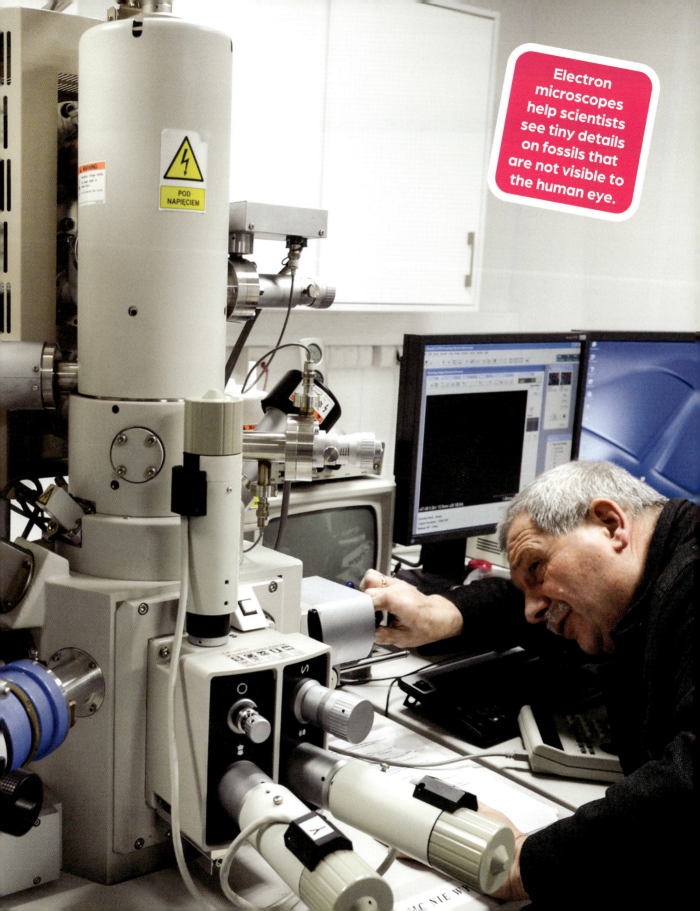

Electron microscopes help scientists see tiny details on fossils that are not visible to the human eye.

Major dinosaur discoveries happen every year. In 2021, scientists learned some new information about how some dinosaurs lived. They found *Mussaurus* (moo-SAWR-uss) dinosaurs of different ages in the same place. Paleontologists found eggs and baby dinosaurs together. They found young dinosaurs together. And they found adult *Mussasuruses* alone and in pairs.

Scientists have found similar fossils in other places. They now know that some dinosaurs preferred to spend time with other dinosaurs of their own age.

Who will make the major discoveries about dinosaurs in the years to come? It could be . . . YOU!

Scientists use technology to create realistic models of dinosaurs.

GLOSSARY

carnivorous (kar–NIH–vor–uss): referring to an animal that eats the flesh of another animal

electron microscope (ee–LEK–tron MY–kruh–skohp): an instrument that allows scientists to see very tiny objects

fossil (FAH–sul): the remains or traces of plants and animals that lived long ago

paleontologist (pay–lee–on–TOL–uh–jist): a scientist who studies plants and animals that lived millions of years ago

predator (PREH–duh–tur): an animal that lives mostly by killing and eating other animals

theropod (THEYR–uh–pod): family of various types of carnivorous dinosaurs that usually walked on their back two legs

WONDER MORE

Think About It: If you had a choice to live in the water instead of on land, would you do it? Why? What would you miss about your life on dry land?

Talk About It: *Spinosaurus* was unique for many reasons. Tell your friends or family what qualities you think make you unique. Ask them about their most unique qualities. Or, better yet, tell your friends and family what you find unique about them.

Write About It: Imagine a world just like ours except that the dinosaurs are still alive. Write about what might happen if humans and dinos had to share Earth. Would they be in conflict? Or would dinosaurs live in zoos with other animals? How would the world be better or worse if the dinos hadn't disappeared?

MESOZOIC ERA

Triassic Period	Jurassic Period	Cretaceous Period
201–252 Million Years Ago	145–201 Million Years Ago	66–145 Million Years Ago

LEARN MORE

BOOKS

Blasing, George, et. al. *Dinosaur Encyclopedia for Kids: The Big Book of Prehistoric Creatures*. Emeryville, CA: Rockridge Press, 2021.

Carr, Aaron. *Spinosaurus*. New York: AV2, 2022.

Kelly, Erin Suzanne. *Dinosaurs*. New York: Children's Press, 2021.

WEBSITES

Visit our website for links about *Spinosaurus*: **childsworld.com/links**

Note to Parents, Caregivers, Teachers, and Librarians: We routinely verify our web links to make sure they are safe and active sites. So encourage your readers to check them out!

INDEX

Africa, 4, 15

bones, 7, 12–13, 18

Carcharodontosaurus, 14–15
Cretaceous Period, 11

Egypt, 7, 11

Giganotosaurus, 15

Jurassic Park 3, 12

Mediterranean Sea, 4
microscopes, 18–19
Morocco, 8
Mussaurus, 20

pterosaurs, 12

Sarcosuchus, 12
Stromer, Ernst, 7

teeth, 4–5, 12, 15, 17
theropods, 11–12
Tyrannosaurus rex, 11

water, 4, 6, 8, 12–13, 15–16
World War II, 7